P9-CSE-487

Wallace & Gromit's Wacky WORLD of KNOWLEDGE

Big Fish

First published in the UK in 2002
by Big Fish, an imprint of
Chrysalis Children's Books,
64 Brewery Road,
London N7 9NT

Copyright © Big Fish 2002
© and ™ Aardman/Wallace & Gromit Ltd. 2002

All rights reserved. No part of this
book may be reproduced or utilized in
any form or by any means, electronic or
mechanical, including photocopying,
recording or by any information storage
and retrieval system, without permission
in writing from the publisher except by
a reviewer who may quote brief
passages in a review.

ISBN: 1 84347 024 1

British Library Cataloguing in
Publication Data for this book is
available from the British Library.

Authors: Neil Morris; Steve Parker
Wallace & Gromit text: Tristan Davies
Project Editor: Jean Coppendale
Designer: Andrew McGovern
Picture Research: Julie McMahon

Editorial Director: Honor Head
Art Director: Simon Rosenheim

Printed in Singapore

Contents

EXPLORING SPACE

The universe is so huge that no one knows where it ends. No one can count the stars in space or know what kinds of life forms are out there looking back at us. In fact, space is so big that a rocket journey around our own solar system would take more than 100 years. First stop, the planets...

All of the nine planets and the Sun are called the solar system. Earth is the third planet from the Sun.

← OUR HOME PLANET

More about this one later!

↓ THE HOTTEST AND THE COLDEST

Mercury is the closest planet to the Sun. Its side facing the Sun is 450°C – twice as hot as a very hot oven. Yet the other side, in the dark, is minus 180°C – three times colder than anywhere on Earth.

← THE RED PLANET

A hundred years ago some people thought that there was life on Mars. Through telescopes, they saw lines which they said were canals built by Martians to carry water to their crops. But the lines aren't really there. Spacecraft to Mars have found no life.

← MORNING AND EVENING

Venus is the brightest planet seen from Earth. It twinkles so brightly that it's called the evening star (or the morning star if you're up before dawn) even though it's really a planet. It reflects sunlight off its brilliant white clouds – which are made of deadly acid droplets and dry ice (carbon dioxide).

STORMY WEATHER →

Jupiter is the largest planet, 1,300 times bigger than Earth. Its Great Red Spot is a massive swirling storm, twice as big as Earth. Jupiter is made mostly of hydrogen gas, the lightest substance of all. You couldn't land on Jupiter - there's no land!

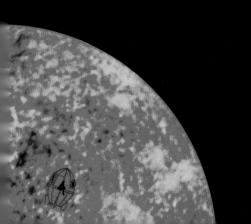

BY GEORGE! →

Uranus was almost called the planet George! It was discovered by English musician-stargazer William Herschel in 1781. He wanted to name it in honour of King George III. But experts said it should be named after a god of ancient legend, like the other planets.

POOR LONELY PLUTO →

It's a long time between birthdays on Pluto. A planet's year is the time it takes for one orbit (once around the Sun). Pluto is so distant that its year is almost 248 times longer than ours on Earth...

THE BLUE PLANET →

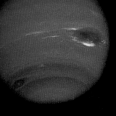

Neptune is the only bright blue planet. Its clouds and surface are a mixture of deadly chemicals such as ammonia. Neptune is a very, very cold place, with temperatures like minus 220°C, because it's so far away from the Sun – to Neptune the Sun is almost like an ordinary star twinkling in the sky.

Shall I pour you a cup of tea, lad?

Not in zero gravity, thanks!

By Jupiter! I've got that sinking feeling!

↑ RUNNING RINGS AROUND SATURN

Saturn's dazzling rings are billions of lumps of ice and rock – from pea-sized to car-sized. The three main rings are 60,000km wide but only a kilometre or two thick.

ASK GROMIT

Do all planets spin the same way?
No. Seen from above, most planets spin anticlockwise. But Venus spins clockwise, and Uranus spins on its side!

Which planet has ears?
Almost 400 years ago, the scientist Galileo studied Saturn through his early telescope. He saw its rings as blurry bulges on either side. He said: Saturn has ears!

MOON WALKING

↓ THE LONGEST FEET

From 1969 to 1972, twelve astronauts landed on the Moon and walked about. Their spaceboots made deep prints in the soft moon-dust. With no wind or rain to spoil them, the prints will still be there in 10,000 years!

It looks a lot smaller than when we last visited, eh, Gromit?

SEAS WITH NO WATER →

Through a telescope, the Moon seems to have seas – these are the flat, dark areas. But they are really dry, dusty plains. There is no water on the Moon's surface.

↓ On the Moon there are rocks, mountains and lots of craters – huge bowl-shaped areas where meteorites (whizzing lumps of space rock) smashed into the surface.

↑ NOW YOU SEE IT...

Seen from Earth, the Moon seems to change shape each month, from a thin crescent New Moon, to a round Full Moon, to a thin, curved Old Moon. But we see only the part which glows bright white because it is lit by the Sun. The rest of the Moon is always there, but it's in dark shadow, so we don't notice it.

BITE-SIZE FACT
You can jump higher on the Moon because you'd weigh six times less than you do on Earth.

IS THE MOON MADE OF CHEESE? ↓

Noooooo! It's made of rocks, like Earth. But the Moon is much smaller, only one-quarter as wide as Earth. Its pull of gravity is not enough to hold any atmosphere (air). So there are no clouds or rain on the Moon – in fact there's no weather of any kind. You can only move about if you're safe, warm and breathing air, in a spacesuit or Moon-buggy.

Crikey! This moon needs a pedestrian crossing!

IN DEEP SPACE

A STAR IS BORN ↓

Here and there in space are vast clouds of dust, called nebulas. Bits of this dust stick together in clumps, which squash into bigger clumps. As the clump grows, so does its gravity, pulling in more dust. Gradually a huge ball forms. The dust in the middle gets pressed so hard that it warms up, glows and catches fire.

Early astromomers ↑ had very good imaginations. They invented constellations in order to identify particular areas of the night sky. They imagined that when certain groups of stars are joined together, they could represent shapes of things like animals or ancient gods. We still use these constellations today for anything from scientific purposes to unlocking our own destiny.

← GATHERED IN GROUPS

Stars aren't evenly spaced in space. They're in groups called galaxies. A typical galaxy has about 100,000 million stars. We are in a galaxy called the Milky Way. It's one billion billion kilometres across, spinning around fast like a top, and shaped like one, too. There are billions of galaxies, with vast empty spaces between them.

↑ Our own galaxy, the Milky Way as seen from Earth.

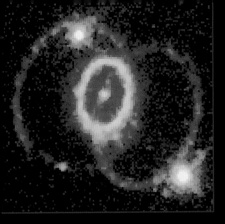

STARS THAT GO WOOF

A big star grows into a supergiant, thousands of times larger than our Sun. But it doesn't last long. After a few million years it goes WOOF, exploding in a giant fireball called a supernova. Every now and then we see a supernova from Earth. Its bright glow lasts a few weeks.

BLACKER THAN THE BLACKEST BLACK →

The blackest place of all is a black hole. It usually forms after a giant star explodes. The leftovers fall into themselves, to take up almost no space at all. There's so much gravity in a black hole, that nothing can escape – not even light. Anything that goes too near, such as another star or a spaceship, gets sucked in and disappears.

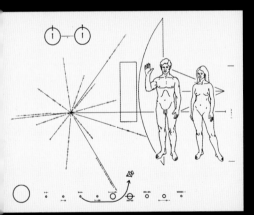

← POSTCARD FROM THE EDGE

In 1977, two space probes called 'Pioneer 10' and 'Pioneer 11' were launched into space with a greeting to any life forms who might understand it. The probes carried a plaque which showed pictures of human beings and space maps giving directions to the Sun as well as indicating where Earth was in the solar system.

This'll give a fair picture of life on Earth!

ASK GROMIT

Are there aliens?
Probably, yes. There are so many galaxies, with so many stars, with so many planets, that life's almost certain to exist somewhere else.

Are we listening for aliens?
Giant telescopes that receive natural radio waves from space are always tuned to possible messages. This is SETI, Search for Extra-Terrestrial Intelligence.

THE SUNNY SIDE UP

BURNING BRIGHT →

Stars are on fire. They make light and heat like gigantic roaring furnaces. But they are so far away, they seem like tiny dots twinkling in the dark night. Yet stars don't just come out at night. They are there in the daytime too. But we have a star which is so near and bright, that its light blots out the distant ones. This nearby star is the Sun and like most stars, the Sun is growing with age – and it's already huge at 1,392,000km across!

Shiff, shiff... I say, Gromit... can you smell something burning?

This is a close-up of the surface of the Sun showing a solar flare with the Earth in the middle for scale.

← THE BIGGEST FIRE

The middle of the Sun is about 5 million°C, which is 10,000 times hotter than a nice log fire at home. Even the surface of the Sun is more than 5,000°C, which would easily melt a teaspoon. Giant flames called solar flares, hundreds of times bigger than Earth, leap from its surface.

A SOLAR ECLIPSE →

When the Moon goes between us and the Sun, blocking its light and heat for a short time, this is called a solar eclipse. When Earth is in the Moon's shadow, it gets dark and cool – and owls may hoot!

↑ WHAT'S A COMET, GROMIT?

The Sun has a lot of gravity. Not only does it keep all the planets in our solar system in orbit, but it also has some distant orbiting visitors called comets. These are small lumps of ice and rock, usually a few kilometres across, that come from outside the solar system, loop around the Sun and head away again, on a long, lop-sided orbit. As comets approach the Sun, the radiation from the Sun creates a tail of vapour and debris that always points away from the Sun.

← SPOTS ON THE SUN

Dark blotches on the Sun's surface are sunspots. They contain incredible amounts of magnetism, which reach far out into space, even to Earth. Every 11 years there are extra sunspots. Their magnetic waves make our televisions and radios go fuzzy and crackly.

ASK GROMIT

Why is a comet like a dog?
It wags its tail! As a comet loops around the Sun, its immense tail swings around so that it always faces away from the Sun.

What's the next nearest star?
After the Sun, next is Proxima Centauri. The Sun's light takes 8 minutes to reach us. Proxima Centauri's light takes over 4 years!

SPACE TRAVEL

← ESCAPING EARTH

The space rocket is the world's most powerful machine, which is why it makes so much noise as it heads into space. To break free from the pull of Earth's gravity, you must speed up to almost 11km every second. This is called escape velocity. If you could go that fast here on Earth, you'd travel right around the world in one hour!

← Space Shuttle 'Discovery'

↓ In the early days of space exploration, the pilots had to carry some strange things with them. In 1961, the Russian cosmonaut Yuri Gagarin made history by being the first man in space. He took with him such things as 'pep pills', a protein mixture and chocolate (back). He even had a butane camping stove (front) in case he landed somewhere unexpectedly on Earth and had to wait to be rescued!

↓ LOOK OUT!

Close to Earth, space is far from empty. You have to dodge over 2,000 objects, from the satellites that give us TV programmes and help with our weather forecasts, to old bits of spacecraft, dead rockets and other bit of space junk. And who knows, maybe even some stray crackers!

← Hubble Space telescope

On re-entry, ↓
a spacecraft comes back into
the Earth's atmosphere.
It goes very fast – 7km
a second – and the outside
heats up to 10 times
hotter than a glowing
coal fire. The special
heat shield which slows
it down and protects
the people inside
is made of special
bathroom tiles!

↓ SPACE HOLIDAY

You can now book the ultimate holiday –
in space. It will be in the ISS, the giant new
International Space Station. It's more than
70m wide and 50m long and there's room
for about 10 people. You can truly
watch the world go by, far below,
once every 90 minutes.

Oh, no!
I forgot to take
the washing in
before we left!

↓ GOING FOR A FLOAT

To go outside a spaceship, you need a spacesuit. This
contains air, keeps you warm and protects you
from tiny, whizzing bits of dust and rock called
micro-meteorites. It's no use trying to walk, with
nothing to push against. The spacesuit has tiny
thrusters, like air puffers, to
move you around.

Walkies,
eh, Gromit!
'space' walkies
that is...

ASK GROMIT

Who was first into space?
A dog! Laika blasted off from Russia in
November 1957, in the spacecraft Sputnik II.

What's the highest telescope?
The Hubble Space telescope, big as a bus, is almost
600km high, going round the Earth. It can see
10 times further than any telescope down here.

What can spy satellites see?
From far above Earth, they can detect vehicles like
trucks and cars, and maybe even people. But the rest
is secret!

OUR HOME PLANET

The Earth measures 40,075km around the equator.

If you were an astronaut zooming through space, planet Earth would look like a blue ball. That's because it's mostly covered by water. Astronauts also see the white swirling patterns of giant clouds. But Earth is moving through space, too – travelling around the Sun at 107,200kph and spinning at the same time at 523kph.

This so-called 'crust', Gromit... is it the sort that would go well with a bit of cheese?

crust

mantle

outer core

inner core

He's gone crackers!

← The Ancient Greeks believed that the Earth was carried on the shoulders of a god called Atlas. The weight of the Earth is 5,976 sextillion kilos – the equivalent of 80 Moons.

← HOT STUFF

The solid outer layer of the Earth that we stand on is called its crust. It's a bit like the peel of an orange. Beneath the crust is a layer called the mantle, which is so hot – up to 1,800°C – that its rocks have partly melted. Further down, at the centre of the planet, is its core – an outer part made of molten, or melted, iron and nickel, and a solid inner core. Here the temperature gets up to 5,000°C – about the same as the surface of the Sun! The distance to the centre of the Earth is roughly the distance from London to Chicago.

Meteors → are small pieces of rock that burn up through the atmosphere as they fall to Earth. They are also called 'shooting stars' or 'falling stars'.

← ALL WRAPPED UP

The Earth is surrounded by a blanket of air called the atmosphere. Without this blanket there would be no rain – in fact, there'd be no weather at all, and no life on Earth. The air gets thinner and colder the further up you go. The average temperature of the air at the ground is 17°C, but at the start of the stratosphere (about 12km up) it averages -52°C – that's 52° below freezing. Brrrrr!

BITE-SIZE FACT
Earth has a very powerful magnetic field. This forces the magnetic needle of a compass always to point to the magnetic north pole – no matter where you are on Earth.

METEORITE ATTACK ↓

There are billions of rocks hurtling through space all the time, and lots of these small meteorites hit Earth every day. Occasionally, a huge meteorite strikes, such as the iron meteorite that made Meteor Crater in Arizona, USA, about 50,000 years ago. The crater made by the crash is 175m deep and more than 1km wide.

So long as it's only a crater... and not a footprint!

Mesosphere
0–80km

Stratosphere
2–50km

Troposphere
–12km

CRACKING AND BUBBLING

↓ Volcanoes are named after Vulcan, the ancient Roman god of fire who made weapons for the gods. His workshop of furnaces was said to be inside Mount Etna – a volcano on the Italian island of Sicily. The volcanic eruptions were thought to be sparks coming from Vulcan working at his mighty forge.

FIERY MOUNTAIN →

A volcano is an opening in the Earth's crust where molten rock, called magma, blasts out. When it reaches the surface, we call the hot, liquid rock lava. Chunks may be flung out like bombs, or sometimes the lava flows out like a red-hot river. Molten lava can move at speeds of up to 100kph.

Don't worry, lad. It's only letting off a bit of steam...

← Scientists who study volcanoes are called volcanologists. When they need to get information from inside the boiling-hot craters of volcanoes, they send in robot volcanologists!

↓ PLANETARY JIGSAW

The Earth's crust is cracked into several huge pieces, called plates. These plates have been moving very slowly for millions of years. Where the plates meet, they push against each other, creating massive pressure. The rocks sometimes slip under this pressure, and this is what causes earthquakes.

↑ After an earthquake, specially trained sniffer dogs search for survivors in the rubble of collapsed buildings. This one is wearing a hard hat and face mask for extra protection.

LIVING WITH QUAKES ↓

Japan lies in a part of the Pacific Ocean where four of the Earth's plates meet. Sometimes the plates rub together, causing underground movements and earthquakes. The ancient Japanese had a different idea: they thought that earthquakes were caused by giant catfish thrashing around in mud!

Good job you don't have to clean the bath after that lot, eh, Gromit?

Some hot springs are great places to lie about in. Just ask these Japanese macaques, commonly known as snow monkeys, that live in Jigokudani, Japan. They come for a daily dip to escape the winter temperatures of −5°C. The water in these springs reaches an amazing 38–40°C. Now that's a really hot bath!

HOT SPRINGS →

In some parts of the world, underground water is heated up by surrounding hot rocks. Sometimes this makes scalding-hot water shoot out of the ground as a geyser. This huge one is Old Faithful in Yellowstone National Park in the US. Just look at the size of the people in this picture!

WET, WET, WET!

Arctic Ocean

Atlantic
Ocean

Pacific
Ocean

Indian
Ocean

The world's oceans contain about 1,377 quintillion litres of water.

← PEACEFUL OCEAN

The Pacific Ocean (meaning 'peaceful') breaks all oceanic records. It's the biggest (area 181.2 million sq km, four times bigger than the biggest continent, Asia), and the deepest (11,022m, over 2,000m deeper than Mount Everest is high). It contains more than half the world's sea water and is dotted with more than 25,000 islands.

I say, Gromit. It's just like being in a giant goldfish bowl.

BITE-SIZE FACT
The deepest human dive ever was made in 1960 in a submersible called 'Trieste,' which took two divers down almost 11km.

← SUBMERSIBLES

Exploring the oceans is very difficult. The depths are dark, temperatures are freezing and the pressure can reach more than 1,125kg (the weight of a small elephant) per sq cm. So scientists use underwater ships called submersibles to explore the ocean floor. These ships allow them to observe, take photographs and carry out a variety of underwater survey and research tasks.

Yes... and now the fish are looking at **US!**

← The Earth's polar regions are covered in masses of ice – in some places about 3km deep. Around the edges, large chunks break off and float out to sea. These are called icebergs and only about $\frac{1}{8}$ appears above the surface; the rest is under water. Over time icebergs melt away, but not before being weathered by the wind and sea into very unusual shapes.

↓ FROM SOURCE TO MOUTH

Rivers are an important part of the world's water cycle. They carry water that falls as rain or snow back to the sea. The longest river in the world, from its source in central Africa to its delta mouth on the Mediterranean Sea, is the Nile. It is 6,670km long and has two main branches, called the Blue and White Nile after the different colours of their waters. But there is a river that contains more water than the Nile, and that's the River Amazon in South America.

↓ The Dead Sea between Israel and Jordan is so full of mineral salts that when people lie in it, they just float about all day!

MOBY DOG

ANGEL FALLS →

In 1935, an American pilot called Jimmy Angel flew over the Guiana Highlands of Venezuela, in South America. He was looking for the mythical city of El Dorado which people used to believe was full of gold. Instead, he found the highest waterfall in the world; the waterfall was named after him. Angel Falls have a drop of 979m. The Empire State Building is 448m tall – so this just shows you how big the Angel Falls really are!

448m -----------------------

ROCK-HARD FACTS

LIVING ROCKS →

Did you know that some rocks were once living? Fossils are the remains of ancient creatures and plants that have changed into rock after being buried by mud millions of years ago.

This is a fossil of an ichthyosaurus that lived around 200 million years ago.

It won't bite lad, it's only a fossil!

Sometimes the wind and rain combine → to make some really strange shapes – such as Wave Rock in Western Australia. This rock is over 27 million years old and has been weathered to make a huge shape like a wave. It's 15m high – lucky it's not a real wave!

← CHANGING SHAPES

The ground under your feet is made up of lots of different kinds of rocks. You may think these rocks never change, but they do. Over many years rain, wind, ice and huge changes of temperature all take their toll. Solid rocks get worn away, and sometimes the spires and pinnacles that are left make bizarre shapes – like these in Monument Valley, Arizona, USA.

PRECIOUS ROCKS →

Some rocks, like rubies, amethysts and opals, are very valuable. They are all minerals called gemstones, which are mined or dug up from the earth. In their raw state, they're not so pretty, but when they've been cut and polished they're often made into beautiful jewellery.

raw opal

polished opal

I can't tell my stalactites from my stalagmites at this angle!

At this angle, I'm not sure I really care...

← WATER DAMAGE

Most underground caves are found in regions of limestone, a soft rock that is dissolved by weak acid. Rainwater is a weak acid because it contains carbon dioxide, which it picks up as it falls through the air and seeps through soil. Over thousands of years, water eats away at cracks and holes in limestone rocks. As the cracks get wider, they make holes and finally caves. Stalagmites and stalactites look like rocky icicles and they are both made by dripping water. They are caused by rainwater seeping through limestone. Stalagmites grow up from the floor of caves and stalactites grow down from the ceiling. When they meet they're called pillars.

Many people think that diamonds → are the world's most beautiful precious stones. Diamond is also the world's hardest natural substance – only a diamond can cut another diamond.

ASK GROMIT

Where were the oldest animal fossils found?
In Australia. Some were of jellyfish and they were as big as truck wheels.

Diamonds may be hardest, but which is the softest mineral?
Talc, from which talcum powder is made.

Who or what are spelunkers?
They are cavers – people who explore caves for fun.

21

He only said 'walkies' when we left the house!

WILD WEATHER

← TWISTER!

Tornadoes are smaller than hurricanes, but they have even stronger whirling winds. The spinning whirlwind of a tornado, or twister, can move fast along the ground and tear up trees and houses. The most powerful twisters have a wind speed of more than 420kph. In the United States, about 800 tornadoes are reported every year.

← IN THE EYE OF THE STORM

The Maya, an ancient Central American people, believed that a god named Hurakan sent storms when he was angry with humans. Now we call violent tropical storms hurricanes. Their winds whirl around a calm area called the 'eye'. Hurricanes are given identifying names, starting with 'A' each year and alternating between boys' and girls' names – like Alex, Betty, and so on.

> The wind's picked up a bit, eh, Gromit?

FLOODING RAINS →

Hurricanes and other storms often cause terrible floods by battering coasts and overfilling rivers with rain. Monsoons also bring heavy rains to parts of Asia every summer and these often lead to flooding. Rivers burst their banks and land becomes flooded, buildings and crops are washed away, streets are full of water and people often have to be rescued.

← IT'S SNOW JOKE!

An avalanche is a mass of snow that slides down the sides of mountains. Some avalanches are so big that they rumble down at more than 160kph. About 600,000 tonnes of snow can fall in one avalanche.

ASK GROMIT

Why does the wind blow?
Because of differences in air temperature: warm air rises, cooler air rushes in to take its place and you have a breeze.

What's the difference between a hurricane, a cyclone and a typhoon?
Nothing – they're all the same.

Which comes first, thunder or lightning?
Thunder is the noise of lightning flashing, and you always see the flash before you hear the noise. Why? – because light moves much faster than sound.

THE LIVING WORLD

The world is full of living things. From the bottom of the oceans to the very tops of the mountains, you'll find all sorts of wondrous plants and animals. But of all the world's environments, none offers a more amazing or diverse collection of living things than the rainforests...

↑ The toucans of the Amazon rainforest in South America use their large, colourful beaks to eat fruits and berries.

Around the world rainforests are being destroyed at a rate of 620 sq km per day. That's an area the size of Tokyo – every day!

↓ SHRINKING FOREST

Tropical rainforests are warm and wet, making them an ideal habitat for wildlife. A tenth of the world's animal species live there. The biggest is the Amazon rainforest in South America, which is more than ten times the size of France. A fifth of the world's bird species are found there, along with monkeys, sloths, jaguars and many hundreds of different kinds of butterflies. But the rainforest is being cleared for farming and mining at an alarming rate, threatening all its wildlife.

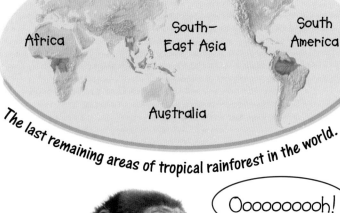

Africa

South-East Asia

South America

Australia

The last remaining areas of tropical rainforest in the world.

Ooooooooh!

← NOISY NEIGHBOURS!

If you visit a South American rainforest you are sure to get an early wake-up call from a howler monkey. Their 'howl' can be heard up to 1.6km away! They live in the canopy, or top, of the rainforest trees and live on fruits and nuts.

Ooh! What a racket!

Yes. It's enough to drive anyone fruit and nuts.

This colourful insect → with its beautiful shiny coat is called a jewel or gem beetle. It lives in the rainforests of the Philippines in South-East Asia.

IT PAYS TO ADVERTISE ↓

Poison arrow frogs live on the floor of the South American rainforests. The amazing colours of these tiny frogs warn predators to stay away, because the frogs' skin is extremely poisonous. They are sometimes called dart frogs, and their poison is used by local Native Americans on the tips of their arrows and blow-gun darts when they go hunting.

COLOUR-CODED CHAMELEON ↓

The chameleon is a kind of lizard that can change colour to match whatever it is standing on or next to. It also sometimes changes colour if it is scared or excited – an angry chameleon often turns black. It has excellent vision, helped by the fact that it can move its eyes independently of each other. And when it sees an insect or other food nearby, it shoots out its sticky tongue, which is much longer than its own body.

← STINKY FLOWER

The Titan arum or giant corpse flower can only be found in the rainforests of Sumatra, Indonesia. The arum can grow up to 10cm a day. The biggest plant ever recorded was around 3m tall. When the flower is in full bloom it gives off a disgusting smell described as a mixture of rotting flesh and excrement. It does this to attract beetles and sweat bees, which act as pollinators.

ASK GROMIT

Which is the fastest growing plant?
Bamboo – some kinds can grow up to 90cm a day!

Why are they called rainforests?
It rains nearly every day in a rainforest! They get over 6m of rain every year, that's about 11.5cm each week.

25

LIFE ON ICE

NORTH POLAR BEAR →

The big white polar bear lives only in the Arctic region around the North Pole. Polar bears are the world's largest land predators and their favourite prey is seals. Female bears usually have two cubs. They dig a den in the snow where they sleep for most of the winter and also give birth. The cubs feed on their mother's milk until they are six months old and stay with her for two years.

← Walruses aren't the prettiest Arctic animal – adult males can weigh more than 1,400kg and their tusks can grow as long as 60cm. But their huge canines are very useful. When a walrus wants to haul itself out of the water, it digs its tusks into the ice and 'walks on its teeth' until it is safely on board a floating slab of ice. Walruses also use their tusks to keep open breathing holes in the ice and as weapons against rivals or enemies, such as killer whales.

I say Gromit, I wouldn't fancy being **his** dentist!

... nor his beautician!

↓ In the polar regions, plants have to make the most of the short warm summer. They have to bloom, pollinate and seed all in two months when the snow has melted.

IMPERIAL UPBRINGING ↓

The emperor penguin is the tallest of the 18 different species of penguins, growing up to 120cm tall. Adult males and females have a space above their feet called a brood pouch, where their single egg and then their hatched chick can be kept warm. Both the male and female take turns to look after the chick in their pouch, while the other waddles up to 100km across the ice to feed at sea. The returning parent feeds the chick by bringing up half-eaten fish in their throat.

I wonder where his other slipper is?

WINTER COATS ←

In most environments, animals sometimes need to be able to hide – no matter if they're a predator or prey. So animals who live in the polar regions need to be able to camouflage themselves in the winter snow as well as in the summer grassland. Arctic foxes and Arctic hares change their grey-brown summer coats to white during winter. Harp seal pups are born with white fur to hide them from predators but this changes to a brown coat when they are old enough to fend for themselves.

Arctic hare

← Where do you go for your summer holidays? The Arctic tern goes a long way! These birds live in the Arctic during summer when they breed, but then they fly 20,000km all the way to the Antarctic to avoid the winter. Wow, just think of all those Air Miles!

Arctic fox

Harp seal pup

ASK GROMIT

Would a polar bear ever catch a penguin?
No! Polar bears live only in the Arctic and penguins live in the Antarctic.

What is the main difference between the Arctic and Antarctic?
The Arctic is frozen water surrounded by land and the Antarctic is a land area surrounded by water.

What is the world's largest animal?
The blue whale, which can grow to a length of 33m and weighs up to 150 tonnes.

HOME ON THE PLAINS

↓ Birds are always on the menu for predators of the savannah. This might be a bit of a problem if you're a bird that can't fly. But ostriches have overcome this. They can escape most predators by being very fast runners. In fact, they can run at speeds of up to 70kph.

NOW YOU SEE ME, NOW YOU DON'T ↓

Grasslands can be found on every continent except Antarctica. The warm, tropical grasslands of Africa are called savannah, and here vast herds of grazing animals find all the vegetation they need to live. In turn, these plant-eaters are a source of food for hungry hunters, including lions, leopards and the fastest of all – cheetahs. As there are few trees or thick shrubs in which to hide, most grassland animals have skin patterns that allow them to blend in with the colour and shadows of their environment. Can you see the two cheetahs below?

KING OF LAZY BEASTS ↓

Lions are experts in lazing about. They spend about 20 hours a day resting or sleeping in the shade. Adult males are the laziest of all – they like to lie around and let the females do the hunting. Lionesses often work in teams to catch antelope or other prey. Then, guess what, the lions find the energy to wake up to eat!

↓ Elephants are the giants of the grasslands. The average elephant is about 4m tall and weighs around 5 tonnes. The fan-like ears of the African elephant are used to keep them cool and also to signal anger.

← Prairie dogs are North American ground squirrels, called dogs because of their barking call. They are very social animals, living together in colonies called 'towns', each of which might contain hundreds or even thousands of animals.

HIGHRISE LIVING →

Termites build huge mounds out of bits of soil stuck together with saliva. Some mounds are over ...m tall and may contain up to ... million termites. Such a huge colony suits termites, because they are social insects. The mound is built by the largest social group, the workers, and is defended by soldiers, which have very strong heads and jaws. At the centre of the mound is a special chamber, where the king and queen of the colony live.

BITE-SIZE FACT
Cheetahs are the fastest animals on Earth. They can reach speeds of 112kph. Lucky they don't get speeding tickets!

Hippopotamuses like→ nothing better than to wallow in water all day long. They only come out of their bath at dusk to graze on grass. Male hippos can open their mouths 1.2m wide and have canines up to 70cm long. Imagine the size of their toothbrush!

Now, this'll have to be the last one... I haven't got any more crackers!

LONG LUNCH →

Giraffes are the tallest animals in the world – they can grow up to 5½m tall. Their necks can reach nearly 2m but they have only 7 vertebrae – that's the same number as humans! Their long necks allow them to reach into the topmost branches of trees such as thorny acacias. Giraffes have extremely long tongues, up to 45cm long, which they use to strip the leaves off branches. Giraffes spend around 20 hours a day browsing in the trees. That's a long lunch!

HOT AND DRY

← FLOWERING STONES

These clever desert plants are called stone plants and look just like stones! This camouflage helps them survive in really hot, dry conditions. The plants store rainwater within their skins, which means they can survive in a drought. In fact, some plants need water only two or three times a year.

Honey pot ants are living jars of honey. They hang upside → down from the ceiling of their nest, where they are fed lots of nectar by other ants. This makes their bodies swell. In a drought the other ants feed on the nectar to survive.

Mind out in front! I can't see what I'm looking at...

← MEET THE MOB

In the flat, open deserts of Southern Africa you have to keep a sharp look-out for predators – from the ground and the air. These meerkats live in family groups called mobs or gangs and they are very good at keeping watch. The meerkats take turns to act as guards while the others in the group forage for food or take a nap. As soon as the look-out gives a warning signal, the whole clan stand tall to locate the danger, before scurrying back to their burrows under ground.

Camels live in regions of extreme temperatures – → both hot and cold. These bactrian camels from the Gobi desert in Mongolia, can withstand −40°C in winter and over 38°C in the summer. And they change their coats to suit the season!

WALKING SNAKE →

Moving around on the hot, slippery sand of a desert can be hard work. But the sidewinder snake, found in the USA and Mexico, travels by moving sideways. It lifts different parts of its body off the ground in turn, so that none of it touches the burning sand for more than a second.

BITE-SIZE FACT
The Atacama desert in Chile, South America, is the driest place on Earth. Parts of it have had no rain for over 400 years. Wow, that's a long hot summer!

DESERT GIANT →

The giant saguaro cactus of the Sonoran desert, in the southern USA and northern Mexico, grows up to 18m tall. Like all cacti, the saguaro stores water in its fleshy stems, some of which grow like candelabra off the main trunk. It produces pretty white flowers, but usually only when it is at least 50 years old. Desert bats, birds and insects gather nectar from the flowers, and other animals eat the cactus fruit.

SAFE AS HOUSES→

The 5cm spikes of the saguaro cactus → help to make it a really safe place to build nests. Birds such as the Gila woodpecker and great horned owl in the Arizona desert seem to think so, too.

Ah, camels for tea, Gromit! Will they have one lump or two, do you think?

UNDERWATER WORLD

SONAR SCHOOL ↓

Most dolphins hunt for their food – fish, squid and shrimps – in groups, or schools, which could consist of hundreds of individuals. Even though they can swim at 30kph, they never bump into each other or lose their way because they use echolocation, a form of sonar, to find their way around. Dolphins also send out clicking sounds, which bounce back off other dolphins, fish, or anything else.

I bet the hammerhead shark is a dab hand at DIY.

I wouldn't want him putting up shelves in our house!

PUFFED UP →

A porcupine fish has a thick, leathery skin that has tiny spines instead of scales. When the fish is calm the spines can't be seen. But when it is angry or threatened a sac inside its body fills with air or water. This makes the fish swell up like a balloon and its spines stick out.

The hammerhead shark is a strange looking fish, but apart from its weird head it's just like any other shark. Hammerheads live in warm, tropical oceans, and the largest are more than 6m long and weigh up to a tonne. They have a reputation for being dangerous and aggressive, but there are very few reports of hammerhead attacks.

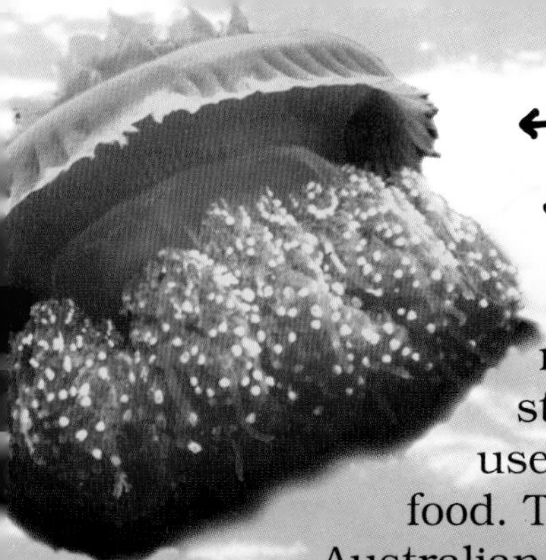

← JELLIED STINGERS

Jellyfish are 98 per cent water and range from tiny creatures to Arctic giants that measure more than 2m across. Most have stinging tentacles, which they use for defence and to catch food. The most dangerous is the Australian box jellyfish, known as the sea wasp, whose sting can kill human swimmers. The Portuguese man-o-war is not actually a single jellyfish, but a whole colony attached together. Their stinging tentacles are up to 9m long.

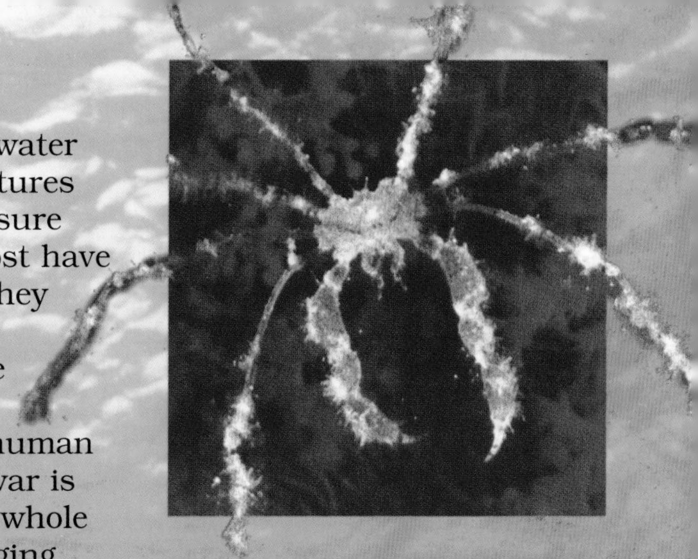

↑ **When you live on a coral reef and want to avoid being seen by predators, you need some tricky camouflage. This decorator crab uses tiny pieces of coral to 'decorate' itself so that it blends into the background.**

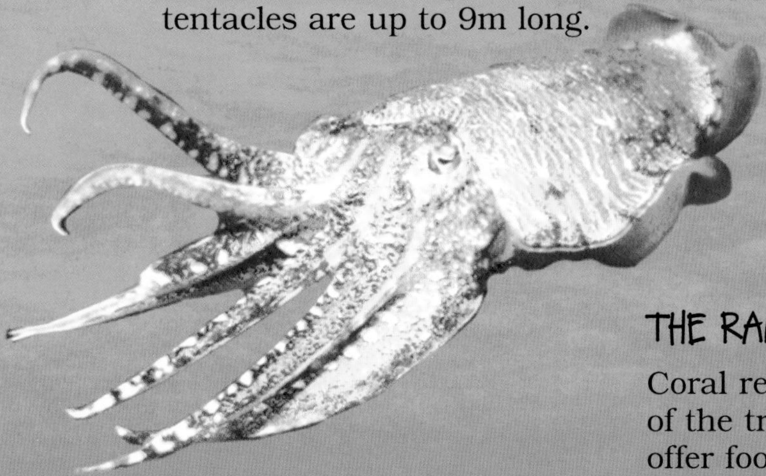

NKY MOLLUSC ↑

'he cuttlefish is not really a fish at all. It's . mollusc related to the squid and octopus. t has eight short arms and two long entacles, which it can shoot out very uickly to catch prey. When it wants to wim fast, it ejects a stream of water and hoots along like a jet. If it is threatened it nakes a cloud of blue-black ink and even changes colour to hide in its surroundings.

THE RAINFORESTS OF THE SEA ↓

Coral reefs are found in the warm seas of the tropics, such as the Red Sea. They offer food and shelter to some of the most colourful and strange sea creatures in the world. Coral reefs are home to hundreds of small fish of all shapes and sizes such as clown fish, butterfly fish and parrot fish. Their bright colours help to hide them against the colours of the coral.

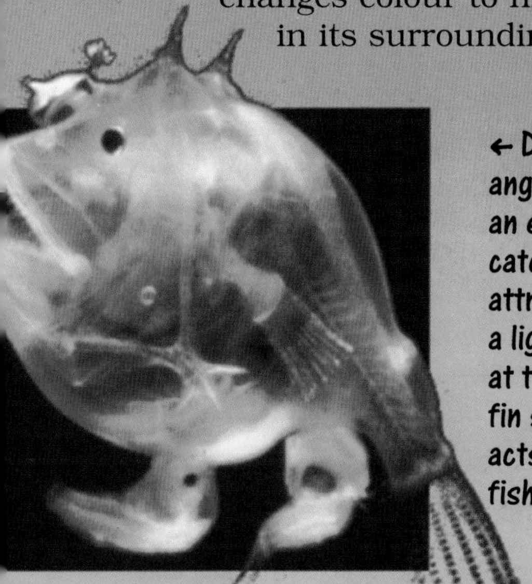

← **Deep-sea angler fish have an extraordinary way of catching other fish. Females attract their prey with a light organ glowing at the end of a fin spine that acts like a fishing rod.**

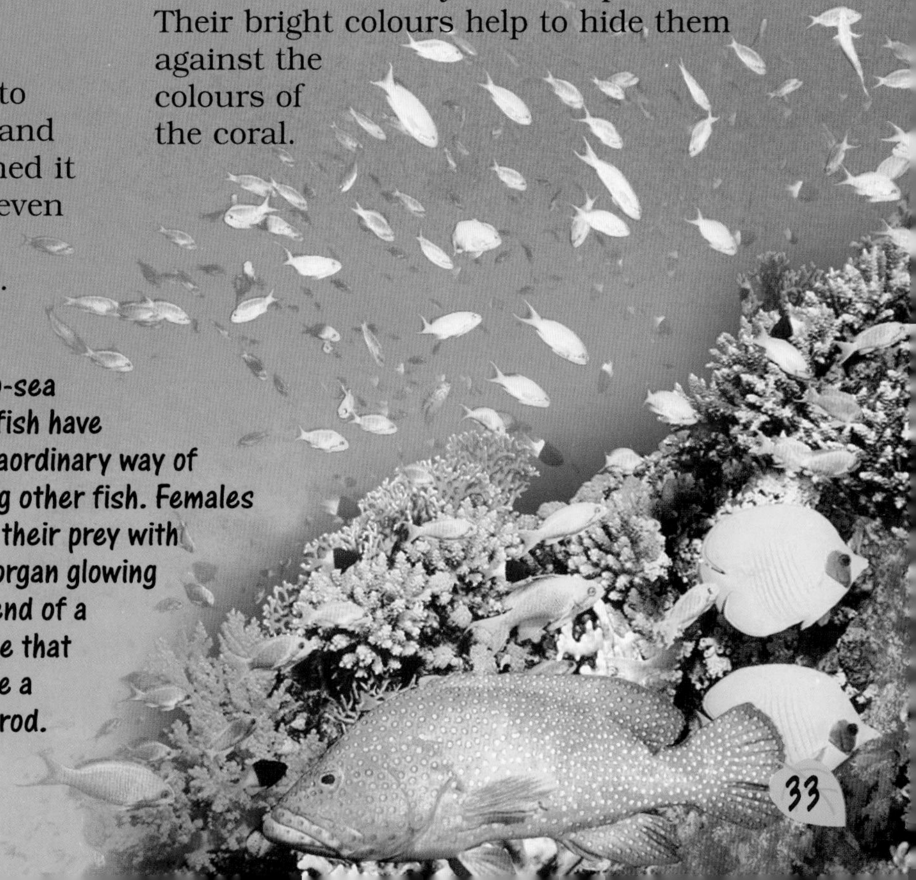

HISTORY HIGHLIGHTS

Some dinosaur eggs were up to 30cm long.

We have a lot of history – from dinosaurs and ancient civilizations to the European explorers who went to the New World. But let's begin with the dinosaurs... The first dinosaurs appeared on Earth about 230 million years ago, and they dominated our planet for 165 million years.

↑ Female dinosaurs laid eggs with hard, leathery shells, often in mud nests. One nesting dinosaur has been named Maiasaura, meaning 'good mother', because scientists think it looked after its young until they were able to fend for themselves.

So long as we keep to the high ground, we can avoid all those prehistoric monsters!

↓ HUMONGOUS HERBIVORE

Apatosaurus ('deceptive lizard') really is a bit deceptive, because it used to be called Brontosaurus ('thunder lizard'). Scientists discovered that Bronto fossils were the same as the earlier named Apatosaurus, which was an enormous plant-eater. It was up to 21m long and weighed 33 tonnes. It probably spent a lot of time in swamps, thudding on to dry land to rake leaves off tall trees. It may have stood up on its hind legs to reach the highest leaves, and even to crash down on smaller predators such as Allosaurus.

MIGHTY MEAT-EATER →

Tyrannosaurus rex (the 'king of the tyrant reptiles') was a fearsome carnivore. It stood up on its hind legs to about 14m tall (higher than a double-decker bus). T. rex was a bighead too: its head was 1.5m long and its huge jaws were filled with sawlike 18cm teeth. It also had a powerful tail, but its arms and hands were tiny and weak – probably because it just didn't need them.

↑ In 1938, a fisherman caught an unusual looking fish off the Comoros Islands in the Indian Ocean. It had a heavy body and was more than a metre long. To everyone's amazement it turned out to be a coelacanth, a fish thought to have died out about 70 million years ago! These 'dinofish' are unusual because their paired fins move in a similar way to our arms and legs.

I don't suppose I could interest you in... er, a piece of cheese then?

TERRIBLE LIZARDS

When people first found dinosaur fossils, they had no idea what they were. Then, in 1841, Sir Richard Owen gave them the name dinosaurs, meaning 'terrible lizards'. Reptiles ruled the skies as well as the land. Flying reptiles called pterosaurs had wings made of skin, with wing spans up to 13m. These fabulous flyers probably skimmed the oceans scooping up fish in their huge jaws.

ASK GROMIT

Why did dinosaurs die out?
Probably because the Earth was hit by a massive asteroid which made a huge cloud of dust that blocked out the Sun.

Did some dinosaurs have feathers?
Archaeopteryx ('ancient bird') had feathers and is thought to be the first bird (which is why scientists think birds are related to dinosaurs).

35

THE ANCIENT WORLD

← The Colosseum in Rome was officially opened in AD 80.

MAPΓΑΡΕΙΤΗΣ

↑ Part of a mosaic showing a gladiator in combat.

GLAD TO BE A GLADIATOR ↑

Most ancient Roman gladiators were prisoners of war, condemned criminals or slaves. Fights were to the death but if they kept on winning, gladiators might be granted their freedom. The Colosseum in Rome was the most famous venue where the fights or 'games' took place, and also where wild animals such as lions and elephants could be kept for fighting. The huge amphitheatre held 50,000 spectators and could even be flooded for mock sea battles.

← BAKED ARMY

Shi Huangdi (c.259–210 BC) was the first emperor of all China. He was a very tough man, but he was afraid of death. He had a special tomb built, so he would be protected even after his death. It contained a model army of more than 7,000 life-size soldiers made of terracotta (baked clay). The tomb was rediscovered in 1974 by workers digging a well.

Is it my imagination or are they following me?

THE ANCIENT OLYMPICS

The Olympic Games are named after Olympia, a sacred site in ancient Greece dedicated to the supreme god Zeus. The Greeks held festivals there, including a sprint race in which the runners carried shields and wore helmets, but no clothes! From 776 BC onwards, the Games took place at four-year intervals, called Olympiads. It was forbidden for women to watch the Games, let alone take part. The all-conquering Romans finally banned the Olympics in AD 393.

I say, Gromit, this is the biggest garden rockery I've ever seen!

← A Greek vase from c.500 BC, showing the sprint race with naked athletes!

LAND OF THE PHARAOHS

The burial chambers of the pharaohs were full of treasures, such as this gold mask of Tutankhamun. Some pharaohs were buried beneath pyramids. The Great Pyramid at Giza is guarded by the Great Sphinx. More than 72m long and 20m high, the Sphinx has the body of a lion with the head of a man. The Sphinx was carved from limestone, and for much of its history the body was completely buried, with only the head visible. The Great Sphinx still holds mysteries, and some scientists think it might be even older than the pyramids.

↑ Stonehenge, on Salisbury Plain in southern England, is a mysterious circle of megaliths (or 'great stones'). This ancient monument was built in stages between 3000 and 1500 BC, but no one really knows what it was for. The stones were probably dragged to the site on wooden rollers and raised with huge levers and ramps.

↓ The Sphinx in front of the Great Pyramid at Giza.

ASK GROMIT

Were the Egyptian pyramid builders slaves?
No, they were mainly farmers who took time off from their fields during the annual flood of the Nile.

When and where were the first modern Olympics held?
Athens, Greece, in 1896.

Were there any female gladiators?
Yes, the ancient Roman poet Statius mentions them.

TO THE NEW WORLD

↓ MAYAN BALL GAME

Many hundreds of years ago, a native American people called the Maya developed a magnificent civilization in southern Mexico and Central America. Each of their cities had a ball court. There, two teams of players tried to hit a large, solid rubber ball through a stone ring set high in a wall using only their forearms, elbows or hips. Though we call this a 'game', historians believe that, to the Maya, it was more of a sacred ritual. After some games, the losing players were killed by priests and their blood was sacrificed to the gods.

Mayan civilization
AD 250–900

That's a hand ball if ever I saw one!

This two- → headed serpent was probably worn by an Aztec emperor or priest as a sort of badge on special occasions. It is carved in wood and covered in turquoise mosaic. Serpents were very important to Aztec religion and were associated with several of their gods.

Aztec civilization
AD 1325–1521

This magnificent headdress ↓ is said to have been worn by the last Aztec emperor, Moctezuma II. Feathers from over 250 birds were used to make it.

Inca civilization
AD 1200–1533

↓ LOST CITY

Machu Picchu lies about 100km north of the Inca capital city, Cuzco. This 'lost city of the Incas' was discovered in 1911 by an American archaeologist in the mountains of Peru. Incas lived here in the last years of their empire, and may have used the city to observe the stars and for secret religious ceremonies. Palaces, baths, temples, storage rooms and 150 houses have all been found there.

Does my head look big in this, Gromit?

← LUCKY LEIF

A Viking called Leif Eriksson, known as Leif the Lucky, travelled from Greenland around AD 1002. He named the first land he reached Helluland, meaning 'land of flat stones'. This was probably Baffin Island, in present-day Canada. He then sailed on to Markland ('forest land') – probably the Canadian mainland. Finally, the Vikings reached Vinland ('wine land'), where wild grapes grew. This may have been the island of Newfoundland, where Viking remains have been found. But some historians believe Vinland was in modern Maine, USA.

> Everything's ship shape and Viking fashion, eh, lad!

Journey of
Leif Eriksson
AD 1002

Journey
of Columbus
AD 1492

← LAND AHOY!

Christopher Columbus was Italian (born in Genoa), but he sailed across the Atlantic on behalf of Spain – because the Spanish monarchs Ferdinand and Isabella paid for the trip. When Columbus sailed west, he thought he would discover a short route to Asia – though some of his crew were convinced they would fall off the edge of the world! When he sighted land on 12 October 1492, Columbus thought he had reached the East Indies so he called the local islanders 'Indians'. In fact, he had sighted San Salvador Island, in the Bahamas.

ASK GROMIT

Who were the Vikings?
The Vikings were adventurers, traders and settlers from Norway, Sweden and Denmark.

Why is America called America?
After Amerigo Vespucci, an Italian explorer who visited South America in 1499.

What was El Dorado?
This was a land that the Spanish conquistadores (or conquerors) hoped to find in America. They never found it but they plundered gold and treasure from the Aztecs in Mexico and the Incas in Peru.

TECHNO TIME

The world of science and technology is constantly changing. It's hard to believe that not so long ago a fast car only went at around 3kph, there were no X-rays or lasers, no televisions or computers and certainly no mobile phones. Today, the number of new discoveries and inventions means that science and technology are moving forwards in leaps and bounds – as the progress of transport will show…

The penny-farthing had a massive front wheel, so it was always in high gear. Going uphill was tough on puff!

↓ LUXURY ON WHEELS

Some motorcycles are so large and powerful they are bigger than cars! They have massive music systems, super-heaters, arm-rests for the passenger and a satellite navigation screen so the rider doesn't get lost. These luxury motorbikes are so heavy, if they topple over, it takes two people to lift them upright again.

I say, Gromit, the only thing missing is somewhere to park your tea and biscuits!

Gears are used in most vehicles, → but you can see them easily on a bicycle. In low gear, one turn of the pedals makes the back wheel spin only a short way. Pedalling uphill is easy, but slow. In high gear, one turn of the pedals makes the back wheel spin many times, so you can pedal downhill at speed.

↓ TAKE-OFF

Planes go forwards by engines – but what makes them rise up? Wings. Seen from the side, a wing has an aerofoil shape, more curved above than below. Air has further to go across the upper surface, so it flows faster, which gives less pressure. The greater air pressure under the wing pushes up with a force called lift.

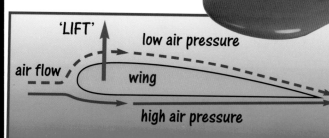

'LIFT'
low air pressure
air flow
wing
high air pressure

BITE-SIZE FACT
Years ago, people thought more wings gave more lift, so planes were designed with 20 or more long, thin wings. These wings were so weak, they collapsed in a heap.

SUN–CARS FOREVER →

Some cars get their energy from Space – from the Sun. A solar-powered car's solar panels change sunlight into electricity for the electric motor. Any spare electricity from the panels charges the batteries, so that when it's cloudy or at night, the car doesn't stop! Solar energy is 'free', but solar panels cannot trap very much of it, and most places are not sunny enough for solar cars to be common – yet.

↓ Bullet trains were first developed in Japan in the 1960s. The 500 Series has attained the world's fastest operating speed of 300kph but has been designed to go even faster at 320kph.

We're going full steam ahead – and I can't even see any steam!

MEDICAL MARVELS

CAT SCAN OR DOG SCAN? →

Scanners make pictures of the body's insides. CAT scanners (computerized axial tomography) use very weak, harmless X-rays. MRI scanners (magnetic resonance imaging) use strong magnetism and weak radio waves. A computer adds up lots of two-dimensional 'flat' pictures to give a three-dimensional view, like a model of the real body.

← ROBO BODY

Some people are part-robot! They have artificial or man-made body parts, such as metal joints, plastic blood vessels and pins and screws to mend broken bones. The latest artificial parts are microchips for eyes and ears. They are being tested to help people see and hear again.

↓ One day, doctors might take a bit of a person's body, and grow spare parts from it, for use if that person ever became ill. It's called cloning. But cloning could also be used to make copies of people. This has already been done with animals, like Dolly the sheep.

I don't know why they clone sheep, they all look alike to me.

I agree!

Well, I don't remember eating **that**!

↑ MAKE NO BONES ABOUT IT!

More than 100 years ago, scientist Wilhelm Roentgen discovered unknown, invisible rays that could pass through flesh but not bone. He took the first pictures of his wife's hand using these rays. Roentgen didn't know what the rays were, so he called them 'X' for 'unknown'. The name stuck – X-rays.

↑ SLICE WITH LIGHT

Surgeons still use very sharp blades called scalpels when performing operations. Another version of these tools is the laser scalpel. Its high-power beam of laser light 'melts' skin and flesh. It can be steered very delicately by tiny amounts, and even focused (brought to a point), to cut within the body, without damaging the outer bits. Laser scalpels are used for delicate areas such as eyes and for pinhole surgery

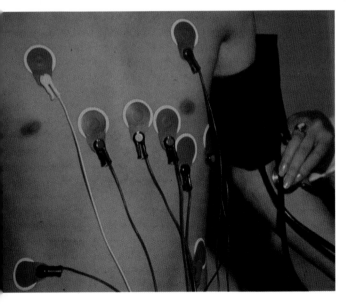

The heart beats every second, 'lub-dup'. It can be heard through a stethoscope, which has a sound tube which is pressed to the chest. Another way to check the heart is the ECG (electrocardiogram) machine. Its sensor pads stick onto the skin and pick up tiny electrical signals sent out by the beating heart. The signals show as wavy lines on a screen or paper strip.

ASK GROMIT

Do we all have brain waves?
Yes. Like the heart, the brain sends out tiny signals of electricity. These are detected by an EEG (electroencephalograph) machine and shown on a screen as wiggly waves.

Does exercise make more muscles?
No, it makes each muscle bigger and stronger. You don't need more muscles – the body already has over 640. But you do need to keep them active and healthy.

Which body part is busiest?
The brain! It doesn't move, but it receives and sends out billions of nerve signals every second. The brain uses up ten times more energy, for its size, than other body parts.

IN THE HOME

← FRUITY TIME

Some fruits, like lemons and limes, contain acids. Many kinds of batteries also contain acids and metals such as copper. A reaction between the acid and the metal makes electricity flow. If you stick a copper wire into a lemon, the same can happen – although the electricity is very weak. This is how the fruit-powered clock (which you can buy as a kit) works.

WHY DO FIZZY DRINKS FIZZ? ↓

A fizzy drink looks bubble-free in the bottle. The bubbles are there, but under great pressure, squashed too tiny to see. When you take off the top, you release the pressure, and the bubbles blow up like balloons. Take off the top too fast and the fizz overflows, so release it slowly.

'How much is that doggy in the window?'

I wonder what time Top of the Pups is on?

← Once there was only live sound, from voices and instruments. People first heard recorded sound from a machine, Thomas Edison's phonograph, about 130 years ago. Some thought it was the 'devil speaking'! Today's sound systems have radio, tape, CD, DVD, even vinyl disc and videotape. These send small electrical signals to the amplifier, which makes them strong enough to power loudspeakers, which change them back into sounds.

MORNING
BIG CHEESE IS
TOAST OF THE
TOWN

This robodog is called AIBO, which means 'partner' in Japanese, and it is one of the most advanced toy robots. It can recognize its own name, growl and bark and respond to commands such as 'sit' and 'walk' via a remote control. It can also kick or head a ball. AIBO has a video camera for eyes and is PC compatible.

I'll just wait 'til his battery runs down!

ON THE MOBILE →

Twenty years ago, mobile phones were as big as house bricks! A mobile uses low-power radio waves, sent to and from a nearby aerial (transmitter-receiver). This local or cellular aerial looks like a long, thin upright box, usually on a tower. A small dish aerial on the tower uses higher-power radio or microwaves to link into the main network.

BITE-SIZE FACT
The first voice message transmitted by radio waves was on 23 December 1900 by Prof. Reginald Fessenden. He said, 'One, two, three, four. Is it snowing where you are, Mr Thiessen?'

Mind where you point that or it'll make even more crumbs!

↓ Does a vacuum cleaner clean vacuums? No. It tries to suck up air and leave nothing – a vacuum. But more air always rushes along to replace the sucked-up air. This flow of air carries dust and bits up the hose. It takes time to get out a vacuum cleaner, unwind the wire and plug it in. To clean a small area of floor, is a dustpan and brush faster?

...now, time for a nice cup of tea...

ANIMAL ANTICS

The blue whale is the **world's biggest animal** – it grows up to 33m long and weighs up to 150 tonnes.

Kitti's hog-nosed bat is the **world's smallest mammal** weighing in at a tiny 2g.

The **slowest animal** is the three-toed sloth which moves at 2m per minute.

The **fastest bird on land** is the ostrich which runs up to 70kph.

BODY BITS

In the human body the biggest bone is the femur, or thigh bone and the smallest bone is the stapes or stirrup bone in the middle ear.

The adult skeleton is made up of about 206 bones but babies are born with 300 bones.

As we grow some bones join or fuse together.

The hairs on your head grow at about 13mm per month, last for 2 to 6 years and then drop out. Eyelash hairs fall out after about 10 weeks.

Fingernails grow at about 0.3cm a month – the longest known fingernails belonged to a man in India and grew to 1.25m long.

EARTH FACTS

Highest mountain peak: Mount Everest, Himalayas – 8,863m
Longest mountain range: Andes, South America – 7,200km
Longest river: Nile Africa – 6,670km
Biggest island: Greenland – 2,175,600 sq km
Deepest ocean: Pacific Ocean – 11,022m

= left; R = right; T = top; B = bottom; C = centre; b/g = background

over (front) Science Photo Library; Chrysalis Images and Digital Vision
ack) Digital Vision and NASA 2 Chrysalis Images 4-5 Digital Vision 6 CL
ASA/Science Photo Library BR Digital Vision 6-7 T b/g Digital Vision B
/g NASA/Science Photo Library 7 TR Digital Vision 8 TL Space Telescope
cience Institute/NASA/Science Photo Library BL Jerry Schad/Science
oto Library 9 TL and TR Digital Vision CL NASA 10 BL NASA/Science
oto Library 10-11 Digital Vision 11 TR and CR Digital Vision 12 CL and
L NASA/Science Photo Library CR Seth Joel/Science Photo Library 12-13
ASA 13 TL NASA CR NASA/Science Photo Library 14 TL Digital Vision CR
immo Jodice/Corbis BL Mehau Kulyk/Science Photo Library 15 L Digital
ision CR Adrienne Hart-Davis/Science Photo Library BR David
arker/Science Photo Library 16 L Wesley Bocxe/Science Photo Library CL
he Art Archive/Museo Statale Metaponto/Dagli Orti CR R.T.
olcomb/Corbis BC Hank Morgan/Science Photo Library 17 TC Sipa
ress/Rex Features CL Digital Vision CR Reuters BL Yann Arthus-
ertrand/Corbis BR DigitalVision 18 BL F.S. Westmorland/Science Photo
brary 18-19 T B & C Alexander/Still Pictures B Ann Purcell/Corbis 19 C
orbert Wu/NHPA BC Digital Vision R Kevin Schafer/NHPA 20 TC Chrysalis
nages CR Gilles Martin/Still Pictures BL Digital Vision 21 TL Elio
iol/Corbis TC Anthony Joyce/RSPCA Photolibrary TR Otto Rogge/NHPA CL
avid Muench/Corbis 22 TR Reuters BL Jim Zuckerman/Corbis 22-23 b/g
eatherstock/NHPA BC W.Bacon/Science Photo Library 23 CR Reuters 24 TL
ichael Sewell/Still Pictures CR Luiz C. Marigo/Still Pictures BL Kevin
chafer/Corbis 25 TL Kjell Sandved/Ecoscene TR Kevin Schafer/Corbis CL
 Martin/RSPCA Photolibrary CR Jacquelinn Kaufmann/Still Pictures BL
eather Angel 26 TC Dan Guravich/Corbis BL Doc White/Ardea 26-27 b/g
onachie/Ecoscene 27 TL Andrey Zvozvikov/Ardea TR Graham
eden/Ecoscene CL Beth Davidow/RSPCA Photolibrary CR Peter Hawkey/
SPCA Photolibrary BL Dan Guravich/Corbis BR M.Watson/Ardea 28 TL CL

and B Digital Vision CR Don Davies/RSPCA Photolibrary 29 TL   and B
Digital Vision C Wayne Lawler/Ecoscsene R Yann Arthus-Bertrand/Corbis
30 TL Heather Angel CR Mantis Wildlife Films/Oxford Scientific Films BL
Digital Vision 30-31 Hedgedog House/Oxford Scientific Films 31 TC
Samantha Purdy/RSPCA Photolibrary BC John Cancalosi/Ardea R Bjorn
Backe/Papilio/Corbis 32 CR and BL Ron & Valerie Taylor/Ardea 32 -33
b/g Norbert Wu/NHPA 33 TL Ardea TR Jones/Shimlock/RSPCA
Photolibrary C Peter Scoones/RSPCA Photolibrary BL Peter David/Natural
Visions/Heather Angel BR Digital Vision 34 TL Robert Harding Picture
Library BL Chrysalis Images 34-35 Chrysalis Images 35 TL Bettman/Corbis
R Chrysalis Images 36 TL Roy Rainsford/Robert Harding Picture Library CR
Edgar Knobloch BL John P. Stevens/Ancient Art & Architecture Collection
37 TL Ronald Sheridan/Ancient Art & Architecture Collection TR Robert
Holmes/Corbis BL and BR Neil Beer/Corbis BC Jeremy Horner/Hutchison
Picture Library 38 TL Robert Francis/South American Pictures TR Chris
Sharp/South American Pictures C Werner Forman Archive/British Museum,
London BL R. Stirling/Ancient Art & Architecture Collection BR Robert
Frerck/Robert Harding Picture Library 39 TL James Davis/Eye
Ubiquitous/Corbis TR Kim Hart/Robert Harding Picture Library CL South
American Pictures CR The Art Archive/Private Collection Italy/Dagli Orti 40
TL Mary Evans Picture Library CL Chrysalis Images BR
Corbis/Stockmarket 41 CR Peter Menzel/Science Photo Library B Michael
Dunning/Science Photo Library 42 TR Geoff Tompkinson/Science Photo
Libray CL James King-Holmes/Science Photo Library BL Reuters 43 TR
Alexander Tsiaras/Science Photo Library BL Science Photo Library 44 TL
Science Museum, London/Heritage-Images CR Digital Vision BC Mary
Evans Picture Library 45 TL Peter Menzel/Science Photo Library R
Lawrence Manning/Corbis

While every attempt has been made to clear copyrights, should there be
any inadvertent omissions please apply to the publisher for rectification.

INDEX